# Mechanic Mike's Machines

# Cars

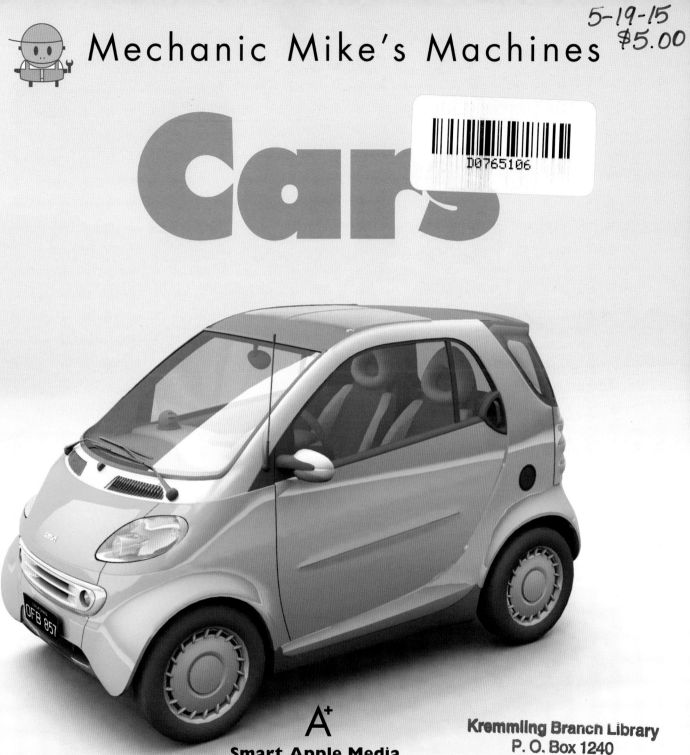

A⁺
**Smart Apple Media**

Published by Smart Apple Media, an imprint of Black Rabbit Books
P.O. Box 3263, Mankato, Minnesota 56002
www.blackrabbitbooks.com

Produced by David West ♁ Children's Books
6 Princeton Court, 55 Felsham Road, London SW15 1AZ

Designed and illustrated by David West

Copyright © 2014 David West Children's Books

Library of Congress Cataloging-in-Publication Data

West, David, 1956-
 Cars / David West.
     pages cm – (Mechanic Mike's machines)
 Includes index.
 Audience: Grades K to grade 3.
 ISBN 978-1-62588-055-0 (library binding)
 ISBN 978-1-62588-094-9 (paperback)
 1.  Automobiles–Juvenile literature.  I. Title.
 TL206.W47 2013
 629.222–dc23
                                2013031984

Printed in China
CPSIA compliance information: DWCB14CP
010114

9 8 7 6 5 4 3 2 1

 **Mechanic Mike says:**
This little guy will tell
you something more
about the machine.

 Find out what type
of engine drives
the car.

 Discover
something you
didn't know.

 Is it fast or slow?
Top speeds are
given here.

 How many people
can it carry?

 Get your
amazing
fact here!

# Contents

**Mechanic Mike says:**
This famous 1929 Bentley
was one of the fastest
sports cars of its day.

GY 3905

# Vintage

Vintage cars were built between the end of World War I in 1918 and the end of 1930. This period is known as the "vintage era".

This car was fitted with a device on the front which super-charged the engine.

This car set a speed record in 1932 at Brooklands, England, with a recorded speed of 138 mph (222.03 km/h).

Did you know that Bentleys are still made today, although they look quite different?

The Bentley could carry four passengers and a driver.

This car had a 4.4 liter gasoline engine with a **supercharger**.

# Electric Car

This little town car runs on electricity. It was originally designed as a gasoline-engined car. Small electric cars are ideal for getting around in towns, where there are recharging stations.

This car has a 74 hp (55 kW) electric engine.

Did you know electric cars are often free from city center **congestion charges**?

The Smart Fortwo electric drive can carry two people.

These little cars are quick, but not fast, with a top speed of 75 mph (120 km/h).

This electric car can travel 84 miles (140 km) before the battery needs recharging.

**Mechanic Mike says:**
Electric cars are more friendly to the environment as they do not produce any exhaust fumes.

**Mechanic Mike says:**
Minivans are also called multi-purpose vehicles (MPVs), multi-utility vehicles (MUVs), people-carriers, or people-movers.

# Minivan

These multi-seat vehicles are popular with large families and many taxi services. Sliding passenger doors make it easier for people to get in and out.

These cars are often fitted with a rear view camera to help the driver see what's behind.

Minivans can be quite speedy with top speeds in excess of 130 mph (210 km/h).

Minivans typically carry around eight people.

Did you know the first minivan looked like a silver teardrop? It was made in 1913.

Minivans are powered by either gasoline or diesel engines.

# Panel Van

Panel vans are just like cars, except that the back half has no windows. These vehicles are used by all types of workers, from plumbers and postal carriers to painters and publishers.

**Mechanic Mike says:** In some countries these small vans are called minivans, which can be confusing.

Panel vans are popular vehicles for airbrush artists to work on.

These small vans have a speed of 90 mph (145 km/h).

These vans can only carry two people.

They use either diesel or gasoline engines. Some have been produced with electric motors as well.

Did you know that every major European car manufacturer has a panel van in their line?

11

**Mechanic Mike says:**
Some countries have their own word for pick-up, such as ute in Australia and New Zealand, or bakkie in South Africa.

# Pick-Up

Pick-ups are similar to sedans but they also have an open cargo area over the back wheels. The cabin area can seat either two or five people.

An ute, short for "utility" or "coupé utility," is a term used in Australia and New Zealand to describe passenger vehicles with a cargo area in the rear.

High performance versions of these cars can reach 168 mph (271 km/h).

Pick-ups can seat either two or five people, depending on the size of the cabin.

Did you know that the ute was the result of a 1932 letter from the wife of a farmer in Australia to the Ford Motor Company, asking for "a vehicle to go to church in on Sundays, and which can carry our pigs to market on Mondays"?

These cars can be powered by either gasoline or diesel engines.

**Mechanic Mike says:**
The first Jeeps were made for the US
Army during World War II.

Jeep

14

# 4x4

Vehicles with four wheels that have power to all four wheels are called 4x4s. Rugged cars, such as Jeeps, can be driven off road over rough ground.

These cars have large tires for extra grip off road.

Did you know that US soldiers gave the Jeep its name?

Although they can travel over 100 mph (160 km/h), these cars are not built for speed.

Jeeps can carry four people and a driver.

These cars are powered by diesel or gasoline engines.

# Sports Car

Sports cars like this Pontiac are small and fast. They can accelerate very quickly, going from 0 to 60 miles per hour in 5 seconds!

**Mechanic Mike says:**
Some cars like this one have **turbochargers** which boost the power of the engine.

16

Sports cars have two doors, two seats, and are very light.

Did you know the first sports car was built in 1910?

This sports car has a top speed of 142 mph (229 km/h).

Sports cars like this one can only carry two people.

This car has a four cylinder gasoline engine.

# Supercar

Supercars are fast, sporty, and expensive. This Bugatti Veyron is one of the fastest road cars in the world.

**Mechanic Mike says:**
When the Bugatti Veyron Sport came out it cost $2.7 million.

18

The engine is so powerful and thirsty that it can only travel 8 miles per gallon (29 liters per 100 km).

 Did you know that the engine is made up of two V-shaped engines and is called a W engine?

 Its top speed is 267 mph (431 km/h).

 Despite its size, it only carries two people.

 The Bugatti Veyron has an 8-liter gasoline engine

# Police Car

This Dodge Charger police car is a powerful machine used by many police departments. It is fitted with sirens, and red and blue warning lights.

Police cars are sometimes known as cop cars, black and whites, or cherry tops.

Did you know the first police car was an electric wagon driven on the streets of Akron, Ohio, in 1899?

Police pursuit cars can reach 150 mph (241 km/h).

Police cars are similar to family sedans, which can seat five. Most police cars have a driver and "shotgun rider".

This police car has a 5.7 liter, V8 gasoline engine.

**Mechanic Mike says:**
Terms for police cars include cruiser, squad car, and patrol car.

21

# Hot Rod

Hot rods are a type of **customized** car. They are usually American cars with large engines that have been modified to go fast.

**Mechanic Mike says:**
It's not just the engine, but all the parts of a hot rod that are modified. This includes suspension, the interior, and even the shape of the body.

Some people think the name "hot rod" comes from "hot roadster," a roadster that was modified for speed.

Some hot rods can reach a top speed of 241 mph (388 km/h).

Hot rods have room for only two people.

Hot rods have a variety of engines, but they are all fueled by gasoline.

Did you know the first hot rods were old cars, such as Model T Fords?

# Glossary

**congestion charge**
Money paid by motorists who travel in a city's central area to keep traffic levels down.

**Model T Ford**
The first affordable motor car. It was first built by the Ford Motor Company in September 1908.

**customized**
Changed to make something exactly the way a person wants it.

**supercharger**
A mechanical device fitted to an engine to make it more powerful.

**turbocharger**
Similar to a supercharger.

# Index